WORLD MYTHOLOGIES

MYTHS OF THE NORSEMEN

Patricia A. Dawson

Cavendish Square
New York

Published in 2016 by Cavendish Square Publishing, LLC
243 5th Avenue, Suite 136, New York, NY 10016

First Edition

Website: cavendishsq.com

CPSIA Compliance Information: Batch #CW16CSQ

Library of Congress Cataloging-in-Publication Data

Dawson, Patricia (Patricia Adelaide)
Myths of the Norsemen / Patricia Dawson.
pages cm. — (World mythologies)
Includes bibliographical references and index.
ISBN 978-1-5026-0992-2 (hardcover) ISBN 978-1-5026-0993-9 (ebook)
1. Mythology, Norse. I. Title.

BL860.D39 2016
293'.13—dc23

2015032451

Editorial Director: David McNamara
Editor: Amy Hayes
Copy Editor: Rebecca Rohan
Art Director: Jeffrey Talbot
Designer: Joseph Macri
Senior Production Manager: Jennifer Ryder-Talbot
Production Editor: Renni Johnson
Photo Research: J8 Media

The photographs in this book are used by permission and through the courtesy of: Werner Forman/Universal Images Group/Getty Images, cover; Paris, France/Archives Charmet/Bridgeman Images, 4; Universal History Archive/Getty Images, 7; North Wind Picture Archives, 8-9, 19; Williams, Morris Meredith/Private Collection/The Stapleton Collection/Bridgeman Images, 10; Leemage/UIG via Getty Images, 13; Prater, Ernest/Private Collection/The Stapleton Collection/Bridgeman Images, 16; Werner Forman/Universal Images Group/Getty Images, 22; Public Domain/Skvattram/ File:Runestone Og211.JPG/Wikimedia Commons, 25; Look and Learn/Bridgeman Images, 26-27; Mary Evans Picture Library, 28; Public Domain/Lorenz Frølich/File:Ymir gets killed by Froelich.jpg/Wikimedia Commons, 32; Public Domain/ Friedrich Wilhelm Heine, 33; Brock, Charles Edmund/Private Collection/Bridgeman Images, 36; A & E Keary, Brock, Charles Edmund/ Private Collection/Bridgeman Images, 42, 59, 63, 69; Becherel/File:The Vikings. Odin Riding his Eight Legs Horse, Sleipnir.jpg/Wikimedia Commons, 43; Penrose, James Doyle/Private Collection/The Stapleton Collection/Bridgeman Images, 44; Eduard Ade and Johannes Gehrts/ File:Thor by Johannes Gehrts.jpg/Wikimedia Commons, 52; Public Domain/Ludwig Pietsch/Wikimedia Commons, 56; Arthur Rackham/ File:Rhinegold and the Valkyries p 070.jpg/Wikimedia Commons, 58; Frederic Lawrence/ File:Frey had seated himself on the throne of Odin.jpg/Wikimedia Commons, 66; Look and Learn/Bridgeman Images, 73; Royal Library, Copenhagen, Denmark/Bridgeman Images, 80.

Printed in the United States of America

TABLE OF CONTENTS

INTRODUCTION

The Importance of Mythology

Odin, the god of war and wisdom, was the leader of the Aesir. This French engraving shows Odin with his crows.

From folk heroes to gods, campfires to cathedrals, **myths** are stories that are told over and over again. These important stories deepen the identity and customs of a culture. Myths shaped the lives of the people who heard them. These timeless tales of a civilization's gods and heroes were a part of the beliefs, values, and practices of people who lived long ago.

What makes a story a myth? Unlike a narrative written by a particular author, a myth is a traditional story that has been handed down from generation to generation, first orally and later in written form. Nearly all myths tell the deeds of gods, goddesses, and other divine beings. These age-old tales were once widely accepted as true and sacred. Their primary purpose was to explain the mysteries of life and the origins of a society's customs, institutions, and religious rituals.

Mythology, the whole collection of myths belonging to a society, played an important role in ancient cultures. In very early times, people created myths to explain the awe-inspiring, uncontrollable forces of nature, such as thunder, lightning, darkness, drought, and death. Even after philosophers and scientists began to develop more rational explanations for these mysteries, myths continued to provide comforting answers to the many questions that could never be fully resolved. People of all cultures have asked the same basic questions about the world around them, such as how did the world begin, what is the purpose of living, and what happens after death?

The myths of the Norse are filled with honor, love, and glory. There is trickery, wisdom, and sacrifice. These myths were not just created out of people's imaginations.

A civilization's geography, government, and culture all influence what stories are told, and which stories eventually become myth. For example, many myths of the Norsemen include wolves, a serious predator of the Scandinavian peoples. They believed the end of the world, or **Ragnarok**, would bring about a never-ending winter, showing the Norse respect and fear of the cold.

Mythology serves as instruction, inspiration, and entertainment. Well-known stories offer people in a society a way to express their fundamental beliefs and values and communicate these beliefs to future generations. Myths preserve and embellish tales of a civilization's accomplishments and teach important lessons about conduct and priorities. These captivating stories provided enjoyment to countless listeners and readers in ancient times, just as they do today.

Odin, the god of war, is shown here in a wood cutting from 1834.

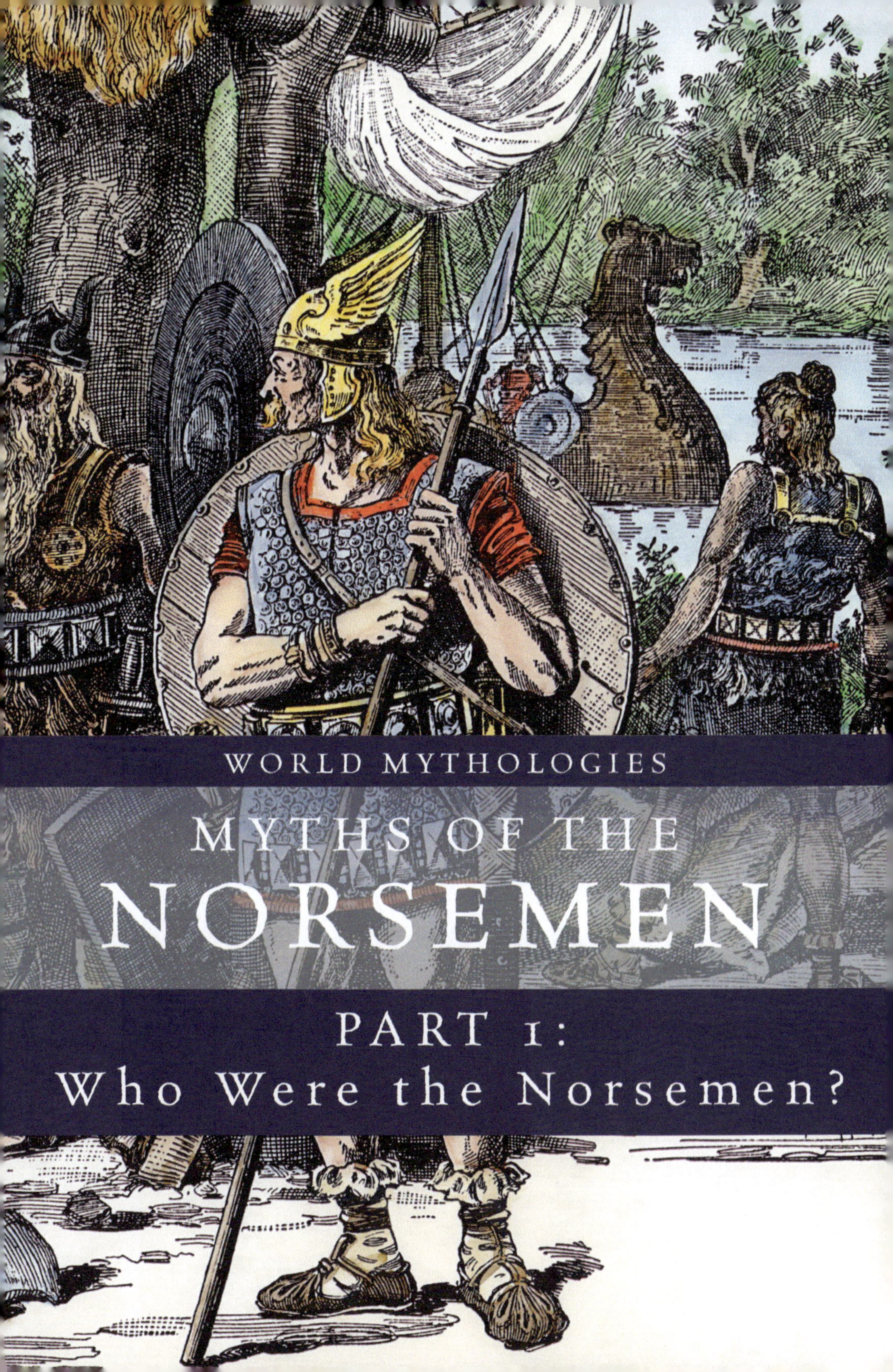

WORLD MYTHOLOGIES

MYTHS OF THE NORSEMEN

PART 1: Who Were the Norsemen?

PART 1: Who Were the Norsemen?

The Cold World of the Norsemen

The cold, inhospitable lands made travel and survival a challenge for the Norsemen

The Norse world was harsh and cold. The Norse people lived in the area of ancient northern Europe known as Scandinavia. Present-day Norway, Sweden, Denmark, and Iceland all made up the Norse lands. The winters there were long and deadly, and the daylight hours were very short. Summers were mild but brief. Even the land was a challenge, rugged with huge mountain ranges, grand lakes and rivers, and high cliffs overlooking the crashing waves of oceans and seas.

The men and women who settled in these inhospitable lands had to be tough. They spent their lives struggling against the cold and dark, cruel storms and howling winds, hungry wolves and fierce neighboring tribes. In a world where almost everything seemed to be against them, the Norsemen came to value courage above all other qualities. They believed that there was no greater glory than to die fearlessly battling the world's evils. They honored men and women who faced life's hardships without bitterness, with a sense of humor and a spirit of adventure. They were intensely loyal to their kinfolk and leaders but also prided themselves on their self-reliance. In battle, a Norse warrior might ignore his leader's commands and charge into danger if he saw a chance to avenge a friend's death or achieve lasting fame through daring deeds.

These hardy adventurers told tales of heroes facing harsh environments and overcoming amazing odds. A common theme in Norse mythology is battling against the elements, particularly against the winter. The Norse gods struggle against forces of evil, which are always cold and dark. Even gods die in the Norse mythology, and the end of the world will come at the final battle at Ragnarok, leaving the world in an unending winter of ice.

Explorers, Warriors, and Traders

In this illustration from a French newspaper, the Vikings arrive in Normandy in the ninth century.

The Norsemen were a loosely related group of tribes known as **Germanic peoples**. Even though they were called Germanic, this doesn't mean that they always came from what is now the land of Germany. Instead, they spread across Northern Europe. The history of the Germanic peoples spans back nearly three thousand years. The most famous Norsemen by far were the Vikings.

Historians have traced the roots of Norse culture all the way back to the Scandinavian Bronze Age, which began around 1600 BCE. During the Bronze Age, southern Scandinavia was home to several Germanic tribes. The Germanic peoples were skilled shipbuilders, navigators, and craft workers. They had no written language, but they left behind spectacular rock carvings and metal figures of gods and goddesses. These ancient artifacts are the earliest evidence of a rich mythological world populated with hundreds of divine beings.

From about the third to the sixth century CE, many of the Germanic tribes moved across central and western Europe in a series of wars and migrations. During this Migration Age, Germanic peoples settled in Britain, France, Spain, Italy, and as far south as northern Africa. Wherever they went, they brought along their ancient beliefs and their tales of heroic kings, mighty gods, and evil giants.

By the end of the eighth century, most parts of Europe had converted to Christianity. In Scandinavia, however, the ancient Norse world of gods and giants endured. A patchwork of small kingdoms emerged, each ruled by a rich and powerful chieftain. To expand their kingdoms, chieftains sometimes led small bands of loyal followers into battle against neighboring territories. Some chieftains also raided foreign lands. Traveling in swift longships, the Scandinavian warrior bands staged hit-and-run attacks on monasteries and seaports in Britain and along the western European coast. The people who lived in terror of the fierce invaders gave them a variety of names, including Northmen or Norsemen. The Scandinavians called their warriors Vikings, from the Old Norse word *víkingr*, meaning "raider" or "pirate."

For more than two centuries, the Vikings built fame and fortune through their raids. Some warriors settled in the lands they had plundered, carving out colonies that stretched over large areas of Western Europe. Viking raiders and traders also ventured east, establishing settlements in what is now Russia. Viking explorers even crossed the uncharted waters of the North Atlantic Ocean in search of new lands. They built large settlements in Iceland and smaller colonies amid the snow and ice of Greenland. Around the year 1000, the Viking explorer Leif Eriksson sailed west from Greenland and became the first European to set foot in North America.

Strong Scandinavian rulers united tribes, and in time three kingdoms began to emerge. These became the lands of Denmark, Norway, and Sweden. Eventually, Christianity made its way into these kingdoms, and the old ways of the Norse began to fade. Raiding and trading expeditions gave way to less perilous pursuits, such as farming, business, and government. Without the superior fighting power of Norse warriors, other powers in Western Europe began to hold influence in the Scandinavian region. By the end of the eleventh century, the Viking Age had faded, along with the culture of the Norse peoples.

PART 1: Who Were the Norsemen?

Life in Scandinavian Society

Scandinavian tenants paid rent to the nobles for common pasture and land. They usually paid this rent with commodities, such as beef or poultry.

Norse society was made up of three different social classes. These were the nobles, the freemen, and the thralls. The noble class was made up of chieftains and superior warriors. There were many ranks and titles, but what nobility came down to was wealth and power determined by land and the number of people under their control. The highest-ranking nobles were the jarls, or earls. These jarls controlled vast estates and commanded large bands of loyal warriors who pledged to follow them on raids and other expeditions. The fiercer the band of warriors, the richer and more powerful the jarls became.

The majority of Scandinavians belonged to the freemen class. This large group consisted of farmers and all other free working people. Farm families typically consisted not only of a couple and their children but also the farmer's parents, unmarried brothers and sisters, and other relatives. All of the members of this large extended family lived together in a long rectangular dwelling called a longhouse. Once or twice a year, the men of the household took part in the Things, democratic assemblies where issues concerning the community were decided. Freemen also might venture away from home to trade or to join raiding expeditions.

Thralls, or slaves, made up the lowest class in Scandinavian society. Most thralls were foreigners who had been captured in raids and warfare. They had few rights or privileges. Slaves worked mainly as manual laborers or household servants, performing the hardest and dirtiest chores. However, slaves with special skills or beauty sometimes enjoyed a respected position in the household, perhaps serving as the manager of an estate or governess to their owners' children.

From what we know, men dominated Scandinavian society. Women belonged to the same class as their fathers or husbands. However, the Norsemen were very progressive for the time. Women had many important rights. Wives had the right to own and inherit their own property and could divorce their husbands. Women also enjoyed considerable respect, responsibility, and influence within their homes. When men went off to raid, women ran farms and homes in their husband's absence. These empowered women were represented in the tales of brave and outspoken women of Norse mythology. The most famous of these were the **Valkyries**, mythic women warriors who were said to lead the souls of those fallen in battle to **Valhalla**.

The Mighty Aesir and More

Frigg, the wife of Odin, is depicted driving a chariot in this hand-colored woodcut.

The **Aesir** were powerful, warlike gods that made up the majority of Norse mythology. They lived in **Asgard**, a beautiful realm far above the world of humans. The leader of the Aesir was Odin, god of war and wisdom. He ruled as king with his wife Frigg, who had the power to see the future. Their most famous child was Thor, a great warrior whose mighty hammer struck terror in the hearts of his enemies. Other famous Norse gods include Tyr, the bravest war god, and Balder, the patron god of light, joy, and beauty.

A second group of gods, the **Vanir**, were associated with fertility. The Norsemen believed that the Vanir were responsible for bountiful harvests, good fishing, and healthy children. Three of these ancient gods lived with the Aesir in Asgard: Njord, god of the sea; Frey, god of the harvest; and Freyja, goddess of love and fertility.

Deities weren't the only mythical beings of Norse tales. A host of other supernatural creatures were revered and feared by Scandinavian people. There were elves, both light and dark; light elves inhabited the lakes and forests, while dark elves dwelt underground. The other creatures of the underground world were dwarfs, who mined for treasure in deep caverns and crafted magical objects for the gods. Then there were menacing giants, killers who lurked in fire, storm clouds, and the mountains.

The most fearsome of all giants were the evil frost giants. The frost giants sent icy winds and deadly avalanches down from the frozen mountaintops. These evil frozen beings hated both gods and humans. It was said that their undying hatred would bring about the death of the gods and the end of the world. This would be the result of the final epic battle, Ragnarok.

FAMILY TREE *of the* NORSE GODS

The two main groups of Norse deities were the Aesir and Vanir. The Aesir were associated with war and destiny, while the Vanir were gods of fertility. The most important gods and goddesses from each group are listed below.

AESIR

ODIN
King of the gods; god of war, wisdom, learning, and magic

FRIGG
Wife of Odin and queen of the Aesir; goddess of marriage and motherhood

THOR
God of thunder, lightning, weather, and crops

HEIMDALL
Guardian of the bridge Bifrost

TYR
God of war and justice

BALDER
God of light, joy, purity, innocence, and beauty

HOD
Blind god of darkness

VANIR

NJORD
God of the sea

FREY
God of sunshine, rain, peace, prosperity, and the harvest

FREYJA
Goddess of love, fertility, and magic

IDUN
Goddess of fertility, youth, and the spring

PART 1: Who Were the Norsemen?

Preserving Norse Tradition

This Borgund Stave church in Norway was built in the early twelfth century. It now operates as a museum.

While the Norse had gods, the Scandinavians' views about religious practices varied. Ideas about the gods varied from person to person and place to place. This was because the Norse religion had no central church and no creed. Yet, bound by heritage, the Norsemen had many traditional beliefs and practices. They also had the same body of ancient myths.

During the Viking Age, the Scandinavians built temples to honor their gods. For most of their history, though, the Norsemen worshipped in sacred groves, forests, and other open spaces. A chieftain or other respected leader led the community in observing public rituals, feasts, and festivals honoring the gods. One of the most important ways to secure a god's blessings was through offerings of food; valuable objects such as tools, jewelry, and weapons; and sacrificial animals. **Archaeologists** exploring ancient Scandinavian offering sites have also found evidence of human sacrifices. One ancient site in Denmark held the remains of several men who had been strangled and stabbed. The dead were probably slaves or prisoners of war sacrificed as an offering to the war god Odin.

In addition to their public observances, the Norsemen worshipped in their homes. A family often chose a god or goddess as their special protector and honored that deity through prayers and offerings. Farmers called on the nature spirits that were believed to inhabit the hills, rocks, and forests, asking for the spirits' help in their day-to-day lives. Warriors offered gifts to Odin before entering battle.

When the Viking kings adopted Christianity, the Christian God became the focus of Scandinavian culture. Christianity gradually replaced the ancient Norse gods. Norse myths had been passed down orally for centuries and nearly disappeared when they gave way to the ancient stories of the Bible. However, the Christian monks, priests, and scholars worked to preserve the Norse culture, collecting traditional tales and recording them. The ancient poems and stories of beauty, humor, and excitement are preserved thanks to these scholars.

A runestone in Sweden carries an Old Norse inscription. Runestones were often used as memorials to Viking warriors.

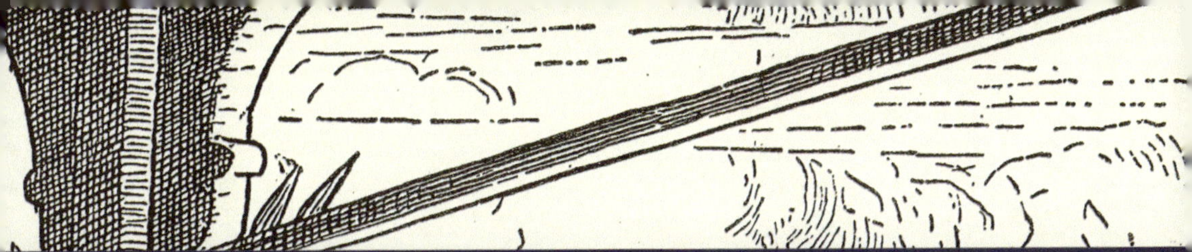

WORLD MYTHOLOGIES

MYTHS OF THE NORSEMEN

PART 2: Stories and Myth

PART 2: Stories and Myths

A Frost Giant World

Yggdrasil, the sacred ash tree, grew through the center of the three levels of the universe.

Many different mythologies around the world have their own origin tales, and Norse myths are no different. They believed the universe was a vast circle, with three levels stacked on top of each other like plates, with spaces in between. There were nine worlds on the three levels. A mighty ash tree called **Yggdrasil**, or the World Tree, grew through the center of them all. This is the beginning of a series of myths. Norse myths are like episodes in a long tale packed with action, drama, and plenty of twists and turns.

Some parts of the Norse creation story are similar to myths from ancient India, Egypt, Persia (modern-day Iran), and other Eastern lands. The early Norsemen may have heard these accounts during foreign trading expeditions. Back home, **skalds** (courtly poets) told and retold the exotic tales, reshaping them to fit the land and character of Scandinavia. Icelandic poets recorded the first written versions around the end of the Viking Age. Their tales were set in a land of fiery volcanoes and massive glaciers, much like Iceland itself.

Our version of the Norse creation myth comes from two sources: the *Prose Edda* and the *Poetic Edda*. The *Prose Edda* is a handbook of Norse mythology written by Icelandic poet and historian Snorri Sturluson around 1220 CE. Snorri was a devout Christian, but he had great respect for the culture of his ancestors. Concerned that this heritage was disappearing, he prepared a handbook that included his own retellings of many of the ancient myths that had been passed down orally for centuries. The *Poetic Edda* is a collection of thirty-four eddas (traditional Scandinavian poems of gods and heroes) composed by different poets at different times, some as early as the ninth century. The poems were written down by an unknown person or persons in Iceland sometime around the end of the thirteenth century. The Norse creation story is found in the eddic poem *Völuspá*, or "The Wise-Woman's **Prophecy**."

Dramatis Personae

Dramatis Personae is a Latin phrase meaning "persons of the drama," or cast of characters. Here are the gods who play a role in the creation story of the Norsemen:

Ymir (EE-mir) First frost giant

Audhumla (OYD-hoom-lah) Sacred cow who freed the first god from the ice

Buri (BOOR-ee) First god; grandfather of the Aesir

Bor Son of Buri; father of Odin

Odin (OH-din) King of the gods

Vili (VILL-ih) and **Ve** (VEE) Odin's brothers

Bergelmir (BARE-gehl-mir) Grandson of Ymir

Ask (AHSK) and **Embla** (EM-blah) First man and woman

In the Beginning

In the beginning there was no heaven or Earth, no sand or sea or grass. There was only a land of frost in the north, a land of fire in the south, and a vast yawning void called Ginnunga-gap in between. Rivers flowed down from the land of frost. They hardened into ice, and great glaciers filled the northern part of Ginnunga-gap. Sparks and glowing embers flew up from the land of fire.

They thawed the ice, making the southern part of the void golden and warm. Then, where sparks met frost, an amazing thing happened. Life appeared in the drops of water and grew into the likeness of a man. This creature was named Ymir, and he was the first of the frost giants.

Ymir fed on milk from a colossal cow called Audhumla, who had also formed from the melting ice. Audhumla fed by licking the salty ice blocks. By the evening of the first day, the cow's rough tongue had uncovered a man's hair. On the second day, a man's head appeared. On the third day, the whole man stepped free from the ice. He was called Buri, and he was the first of the gods.

In time, Buri had a fine son named Bor. Bor married a giantess, and the couple had three sons, Odin, Vili, and Ve. The sons of Bor were handsome and strong and good. But Ymir, the frost giant, also had sons, and they were monstrous and evil. As might be expected, the two sides did not get along. In time their rivalry led to a battle. Odin and his brothers proved the more powerful. They slew Ymir, and so much blood poured from the old ogre's wounds that the whole family of giants nearly drowned. Only the wise giant Bergelmir escaped. Grabbing his wife, he climbed into his boat, and they rode out the flood in safety. From Bergelmir and his wife would spring all the families of giants.

After the sons of Bor killed Ymir, they rolled him into the great void of Ginnunga-gap. Then they created the world from the giant's body. They pounded and pulled his flesh to fashion the Earth, with all its hills and plains and valleys. They made the mountains from his bones, the rocks and pebbles from his teeth, and the grass from his curly hair. They

Ymir is killed by Odin and his brothers.

circled the Earth with the blood from Ymir's wounds, forming an ocean so vast that the very idea of crossing it would strike most men as impossible.

Next the gods took the giant's skull and raised it over the Earth to make the sky. They tossed his brains into the dome to make the billowing clouds. Then they gathered sparks from the land of flame to give light to the heavens. They placed the sun and moon and stars in the sky, fixing some in place and assigning others a path to travel.

Odin and his brothers were proud of their marvelous craftsmanship. The Earth and sky were beautiful. But somehow the universe still seemed empty. One day, as the gods were walking along the seashore, they came across two fallen trees. With his great powers, Odin raised the trees and breathed the spirit of life into them. Vili gave them movement and understanding.

> They took Ymir and bore him into the middle of the Yawning Void, and made of him the earth.
>
> ~ Snorri Sturluson, The *Prose Edda*

Ve bestowed the gifts of sight, speech, and hearing. When the brothers' work was finished, the new beings no longer looked like trees but like smaller versions of the gods themselves. Odin named the man Ask ("Ash") and the woman Embla ("Elm"). From this first man and woman all the races of men are descended.

The gods knew that all creatures need their own lands to settle. So they took Ymir's eyebrows and built a tall enclosure around the center of the Earth. They named this fortress **Midgard** and gave it to Ask and Embla for their home. They gave the land of Nidavellir ("Dark Fields") to the dwarfs, cunning creatures they had made from the maggots that bred in the Earth. They set aside **Niflheim**, below Midgard, for the dead. They gave **Jotunheim**, land

Odin aims his spear at the open mouth of Fenrir the wolf. Thor raises a shield in defense of the serpent.

on the far edge of the ocean, to the giants. **Muspellheim**, the land of fire, went to a fire giant named Surt, who guarded it with his flaming sword. The gods also fashioned other worlds, for the dark elves, the light elves, and the race of gods known as the Vanir.

> An ash I know,
> Yggdrasil its name …
> Green by [the] well
> does it ever grow
>
> ~ *Voluspa*, The *Poetic Edda*

Last of all, the gods built a stronghold for themselves above Midgard. They named it Asgard, or "Home of the Aesir." Here, Odin sat on his high seat, watching over the nine worlds. He knew all that happened and understood all that he saw. Here Odin's wife Frigg and all his sons and daughters dwelt in magnificent halls with roofs of gold and rooms beyond number. There were twelve divine gods and twelve divine goddesses. All were sacred and powerful. But Odin was the highest of them all, and the others honored him as children do their father. So that Odin and his kindred could visit the world of humans, they built a bridge called **Bifrost**, connecting Asgard and Midgard. You have probably seen this marvelous flaming bridge, but you may call it the rainbow.

Supporting all the regions of the world was Yggdrasil, the greatest of all trees. This mighty ash had three immense roots, reaching into Asgard, Jotunheim, and Niflheim. It was tended by three fair maidens called the **Norns**. Each day these maidens, whose names were Past, Present, and Future, drew water from the Spring of Destiny, which flowed under the root in Asgard. They

The Sibling Sun and Moon

In the *Prose Edda*, Snorri Sturluson explains that our system of measuring the days and years began when the gods gave some of the heavenly bodies paths to travel. Odin and his brothers made special horse-drawn chariots to guide the sun and moon along their assigned paths. Then they visited the world of men to find drivers for their magical chariots.

> There was a man called Mundilfari who had two children. They were so fair and beautiful that he called one of them Moon and the other, a daughter, Sun. ... The gods, however, were angered at his arrogance and took the brother and sister and put them up in the sky. They made Sun drive the horses which drew the chariot of the sun that the gods had made to light the worlds. ... Moon governs the journeying of the moon and decides the time of its waxing and waning. ... [Sun] goes at a great pace; her pursuer is close behind her and there is nothing she can do but flee. ... There are two wolves, and the one pursuing her who is called Skoll [Treachery] is the one she fears; he will catch her [at the end of the world]. The other that runs in front of her, however, is called Hati [Hater] ... and he wants to catch the moon and will in the end.

sprinkled the sacred water on the root of the tree so that its branches would not wither.

The great World Tree held together these nine worlds, and the divine Aesir watched over and held councils in the realms of the heavens. So began the Golden Age, a time of peace and plenty.

The Golden Age Ends

Frey and Freyja, gods of the Vanir, are shown as two forms that come floating through the clear sky.

The Golden Age was a time of peace and plenty, but it came to an end with the universe's first war. Surprisingly, the first war was between the Aesir, the gods of war, and the Vanir, the gods of fertility who lived in the land of Vanaheim. The battle lasted ages, long years of hardship and battle. It ended only when the gods grew weary of fighting and declared a truce. In order to make sure the peace continued, a few of the Vanir came to live with the Aesir in Asgard. Some of the most famous divine immigrants included Njord, god of the sea; Frey, god of the harvest; and Freyja, goddess of love and fertility.

The myth "Rebuilding the Wall of Asgard," reveals that the barrier that once surrounded the home of the Aesir was destroyed during the great war. A giant disguised as a stonemason offers to build a new wall for a high price: the sun, the moon, and the goddess Freyja. The gods scheme to gain the builder's work for free, but their plans soon unravel, with results that are nearly disastrous. Our retelling of this story is based on Snorri Sturluson's *Prose Edda*, the only surviving source that contains the complete myth.

The story of Asgard's wall is one of the first episodes in a series of Norse myths revolving around the hostility between the gods and giants. In these tales the gods represent the forces of order and good, while the giants stand for chaos and evil. If the giant stonemason succeeds in taking the sun, the moon, and Freyja, he will plunge the Earth into eternal darkness, bringing an end to the natural order of the seasons.

This myth also introduces one of the most complex and entertaining characters in Norse mythology, Loki. This unpredictable trickster is the son of a giant, but he lives with the gods in Asgard. Loki is handsome, clever, and mischievous. His cunning schemes place the gods in many difficult situations. However, he is also famous for using his wits to rescue them from their predicaments.

Dramatis Personae

Freyja (FRAY-yuh) Goddess of love and fertility

Loki (LOW-kee) Trickster who lives in Asgard

Svadilfari (SVAHD-ill-fah-ree) Stallion who fathered Sleipnir

Thor God of thunder and lightning

Odin (OH-din) King of the gods

Sleipnir (SLAPE-nir) Odin's eight-legged horse

Rebuilding the Wall of Asgard

The gods were uneasy. The terrible war between the Aesir and Vanir had left the great wall around Asgard in ruins. That left the stronghold of the gods wide open to attacks from the evil rock giants and frost giants. Still, despite the danger, no one volunteered for the wearisome job of rebuilding the massive wall.

One day a stonemason rode across the flaming bridge Bifrost on a magnificent stallion. The man offered to build a new wall, stronger and higher than ever. He would build such a wall that the realm of the gods would stay safe even if the giants stormed their way right up to Asgard's borders. But the mason demanded a heavy price for his services: the hand of the goddess Freyja in marriage and the sun and the moon as a bonus.

The gods were outraged by the mason's presumption. Freyja was wise and beautiful, the most renowned of all the goddesses. How dare a lowly builder even dream of marrying such a radiant being! As they spluttered and shouted, Loki's voice rose above the clamor. With a cunning smile, the trickster pointed out that it would take a year or more for the stonemason to build such a splendid structure. Why not agree to the man's terms, on the condition that he complete the task in a single winter? On the first day of summer, with the job still unfinished, the builder would forfeit his prize, and the gods would gain part of a wall in the bargain.

What a brilliant idea! The gods took Loki's advice and presented the offer to the mason. The man agreed to strike the bargain, but only if his horse, Svadilfari, could help with the building. The gods looked at Loki. The sly one winked and shrugged. And so the gods and the mason took solemn oaths to bind them to their contract.

The first day of winter arrived, and the mason went right to work. Soon the gods were sorry they had listened to Loki. The builder's great stallion was more powerful than anyone could have imagined. Each night Svadilfari hauled incredibly huge boulders to his master. The next day the man shaped the rocks and fit them into the wall. As the weeks flew by, the stronghold grew higher and longer. The snows of winter began to melt, and the job neared completion. Three days before the start of summer, all that remained to build was the gateway, which the mason would surely complete on time with the help of his marvelous stallion.

> [The stonemason] demanded as wages that he should have possession of Freyja, and would fain have had the sun and the moon.
>
> ~ Snorri Sturluson, The *Prose Edda*

Now the gods called another meeting. They debated for hours but could find no way out of their dilemma. The oaths they had taken were sacred. Breaking them would bring dishonor. Whose idea had it been, anyway, to accept that dreadful bargain and risk losing the sun and moon and Freyja? Slowly all eyes turned to Loki. With a deadly shout, all the gods swooped down on the troublemaker. Loki was scared out of his wits! Begging for mercy, he swore that, no matter what it cost him, he would make sure the mason lost his wages.

That evening, as the builder led his stallion toward the rock quarry, a dainty white horse trotted from the woods and whinnied invitingly. Loki had used his magical powers to change himself into a mare! One look at the lovely female and Svadilfari broke free from his master. The mare raced away and the stallion followed, with the builder lumbering after them. All that night the two horses galloped madly among the trees. No stones were hauled, and the mason could not work on the gateway.

The next two evenings, the mare appeared again. Once more there was no building. By the morning of

The Norse Trickster Loki

The trickster is a common figure in mythology. The ancient Greeks, the Native Americans, and a number of other ancient peoples told stories about these contradictory characters who were sometimes charming and mischievous, sometimes cunning and cruel. Many tricksters were shape-shifters, able to take on the form of an animal or another person. Some could even change from male to female and give birth to children. Here is how the *Prose Edda* introduces Loki, one of the most famous mythological tricksters.

> Also reckoned amongst the gods is one that some call the mischief-monger of the Aesir and the father-of-lies and the disgrace-of-gods-and-men. He is the son of the giant Fárbauti and his name is Loki. ... Loki is handsome and fair of face, but has an evil disposition and is very changeable of mood. He excelled all men in the art of cunning, and he always cheats. He was continually involving the Aesir in great difficulties and he often helped them out again by guile.

the third day, the mason could see that he would never finish his work on time. He knew that the gods had tricked him. Seething with anger, he swelled up larger and larger, until suddenly he erupted. His disguise burst, and the gods saw that the stonemason was really a big, hulking, bellowing rock giant!

At the sight of their age-old enemy, the gods forgot their oaths. They hollered for Thor, and the thunder god came running with his mighty hammer. Thor paid the

Loki is lifted from the ground by a gigantic eagle.

builder his wages, but it wasn't the sun and the moon and the goddess. Instead, the god cracked the rock giant's head open with a single blow from his hammer. Then Odin sent the giant down to Niflheim, where the souls of the dead dwell in darkness.

Once the giant was taken care of, the gods finished the wall around Asgard. The summer months passed, and still there was no sign of Loki, who had not returned after transforming into a mare. Then, one day the trickster reappeared, leading a beautiful gray colt with eight spindly legs. As a mare, Loki had given birth to the son of the stallion! In order to make amends with the gods for his part in convincing them to make a deal with the giant mason, Loki gave the marvelous colt to Odin. The king of gods named the colt Sleipnir. Sleipnir grew to become the fastest horse in the universe, carrying his master through the air, across the sea, and even down to the realm of the dead.

Thor paid the builder his wages, and it was not the sun and moon.

~ Snorri Sturluson,
The *Prose Edda*

Odin is depicted on his eight-legged horse, Sleipnir.

PART 2: Stories and Myths

The Gift of Idun

Idun saved her apples for the gods, which give them eternal youth

Many religions and myths have a fertility goddess, one who was responsible for the crops growing or children being born. Idun, whose name means "rejuvenator" or "renewer," was a Norse goddess of youth and fertility. Many believe that she was originally one of the Vanir. The Aesir welcomed her for her sweetness and beauty. When she moved to Asgard she brought a wonderful gift. Idun had a basket of golden apples, and whoever ate one of her apples was given eternal youth.

Idun reserved her apples for the gods and goddesses of Asgard. Naturally, that infuriated the giants, who wanted the gift of youth for themselves. In "Idun and the Magic Apples," a giant kidnaps the goddess and takes her to his mountain home in the north. Robbed of Idun's treasures, the Aesir become old and gray. As often happens in Norse mythology, it turns out that Loki the trickster was behind the gods' crisis, and it is Loki who must save them from their fate.

To the ancient Norsemen, this story might have explained the natural cycle of the seasons. When the golden goddess of youth is carried away to the frozen north, the winter winds howl and even the gods wither. Then Loki sweeps in like the south wind to restore Idun, along with all the beauty and renewal of spring. The myth also tells us why, unlike humans, the gods never grow old.

The myth of Idun's apples is found in two sources. Snorri Sturluson gives us the more recent version in the *Prose Edda*. Snorri based his retelling partly on a poem called *Haustlöng*, or "Autumn-Long," which was composed by Thjódólf of Hvin around the late ninth century. Thjódólf was skald, or court poet, to Harald Fairhair, the first king of a united Norway.

Dramatis Personae

Odin (OH-din) King of the gods

Loki (LOW-kee) Trickster who lives in Asgard

Hoenir (HY-nir) Brother of Odin; sometimes known as Vili

Thiassi (THY-ah-see) Giant who kidnaps Idun

Idun (IH-doon) Goddess of youth, fertility, and the spring

Freyja (FRAY-yuh) Goddess of love and fertility

Heimdall (HAME-doll) Guardian of the bridge Bifrost

Idun and the Apples

One fine summer morning, Odin, Loki, and Hoenir went exploring in the world of humans. All day long, the three gods rambled across Midgard, climbing tall mountains and hiking through stony deserts. By the time the chariot of the sun reached the western sky, their bellies were rumbling with hunger. Peering down into a green valley, the gods saw a herd of oxen. They killed a hefty ox, built a roaring fire, and placed the meat in the flames to cook it. Mouths drooling, they waited. After a time they pulled their supper out of the fire, but to their surprise, the meat was not ready. Again they built up the flames. They waited and waited. But when they tried the meat a second time, it was still raw. At that, Odin the wise declared, "There is dark magic at work here." And a voice above their heads answered, "It is my doing."

Gazing up in surprise, the companions saw a gigantic eagle perched in an oak tree. "Give me my fill of the ox, and I will let the fire cook it," said the eagle. The hungry gods agreed to the bargain. But when the bird sailed down from the tree and seized nearly the whole carcass, Loki grew angry. Grabbing a long, pointed stick, he stabbed the greedy creature. The bird flew up into the air with the weapon lodged in its breast. Then Loki found to his horror that his hands were stuck by magic to the other end of the stick.

Swiftly, the eagle coursed over the ground. It flew just low enough for Loki's legs to slam into every rock, tree stump, and thornbush. The desperate trickster felt as though his arms were being pulled from their sockets. He cried out to the eagle, begging for mercy. Then the great bird, who was really the giant Thiassi in disguise, said that he would let his victim go, on one condition. Loki must swear an oath to bring the goddess Idun and her apples of youth out of Asgard.

In a heartbeat, the trickster agreed. Just as quickly, the giant released him, and Loki tumbled to the ground. With a few curses, he picked himself up and limped back to Asgard. There he paid a visit to Idun's garden, where sweet birds sang and fragrant flowers bloomed in an eternal spring. The fair goddess was sitting beside a clear pool, a basket of shining apples in her lap. Smiling charmingly, Loki told Idun that he had found a wondrous tree just outside Asgard's borders. "It bears golden apples that look much like yours," said the trickster. "I will gladly show you the spot. Why not bring your basket, so that you may compare the fruit to your own apples?"

The young and trusting goddess gladly agreed. She gave Loki her hand, and the schemer led her out from the shelter of her garden, across the rainbow bridge Bifrost. The moment Idun set foot in Midgard, Thiassi swooped down on eagle's wings. Seizing the frightened girl with his claws, he leaped back into the sky. Then he carried her away to his home in the northern mountains.

> All [the gods] became old and grey in their assembly.
>
> ~ Thjódólf of Hvin, *Haustlöng*

The next morning Odin found a gray hair on his pillow. Freyja gazed in her mirror and shrieked when she saw her first wrinkle. All the gods and goddesses hurried to Idun's garden for a bite of her enchanted apples. What they saw there made their hearts sink. Not only was the goddess missing, but the birds had fallen silent and all the lovely flowers were wilting.

That summer was the gloomiest ever in Asgard. Day by day, the Aesir watched their youth and vitality fade away. Their hair turned gray. Their skin sagged and wrinkled. Their backs bent, and their limbs grew stiff and weary. At last Odin called an assembly. The once-mighty gods and goddesses shuffled to their thrones and spoke with trembling voices. Where could Idun have gone? Who had been the last to see her? Finally, Heimdall the watchman thumped the ground with his cane. "My memory is not what it used to be," he said, "but I believe that I last saw her crossing Bifrost, with Loki."

Roaring like an aged bear, Odin called for Loki's capture. The scoundrel was dragged before the assembly, and all the gods and goddesses quarreled over who should have the first chance to torture him. The frightened trickster fell to his knees, swearing that he would somehow retrieve Idun and her apples. He begged Freyja to lend him her magic feather coat, which she sometimes used to visit the land of the dead. Loki put on the coat and turned into a falcon. With a rude squawk, the little bird took off and flew north toward the land of giants.

All this time Idun had been pining away in the icy mountain home of Thiassi. Each day, the giant demanded a bite of her magic apples. Each night, he stormed and raged because she refused him. One morning Thiassi went hunting, leaving the unhappy goddess locked in a small, chilly room. Suddenly, Loki whisked through the window. Landing on Idun's shoulder, he murmured magic words that Odin had given him and transformed her into a tiny brown nut. Then the little bird picked up the nut with his claws and headed back toward Asgard as fast as his wings could carry him.

When Thiassi came home and discovered that Idun was gone, he let out a howl that shook the snow from the mountaintops. The giant hurled himself into the air. He flapped his mighty eagle wings and hurried after the falcon. Back in Asgard, Odin looked up from his high seat. His far-seeing eyes spied the falcon and the giant eagle gaining on him. Odin shouted for the gods to pile wood shavings just inside Asgard's wall. The moment

Loki sped over the wall, they thrust a torch into the fuel. The flames roared skyward. The huge eagle was caught in the blaze. His feathers caught fire, and Thiassi the giant plunged to the ground, where the gods took great pleasure in slaying him.

After the commotion died down, Loki placed the nut on the ground. He said the magic words, and Idun stood before them. With a radiant smile, the goddess held up her basket of apples. As the Aesir tasted the fruit, the years melted away, and once more they stood strong and young and handsome.

The gods held a splendid feast to celebrate Idun's return and the restoration of their youth. Then Odin, who was too happy to continue to hold his grudge, threw Thiassi's eyes into the sky. There they would shine as two bright stars in the night.

Odin's Wisdom

Many Norse myths tell of the wisdom of Odin. The king of gods was said to have spoken to the dead, plucked out one of his eyes, and even hanged himself on Yggdrasil in his endless quest for knowledge. The story of Odin's sacrifice on the World Tree is related in the poem *Hávamál*, which translates to "The Speech of the High One," from the collection of traditional Scandinavian poems known as the *Poetic Edda*. In this excerpt from *Hávamál*, Odin explains that he sacrificed himself in order to learn the secret of **runes.** Runes were the characters, or letters, of the alphabet of the early Scandinavians. Used in short inscriptions on wood, stone, and other hard surfaces, they were often believed to have magical powers.

I know that I hung,
on a wind-rocked tree,
nine whole nights,
with a spear wounded,
and to Odin offered,
myself to myself;
on that tree,
of which no one knows
from what root it springs.

Bread no one gave me,
nor a horn of drink,
downward I peered,
to runes applied myself,
wailing learnt them,
then fell down thence. ...

Then I began to bear fruit,
and to know many things,
to grow and well thrive:
word by word
I sought out words,
fact by fact
I sought out facts.

PART 2: Stories and Myths

Recovering the Mjollnir

Thor rides his chariot pulled by goats while wielding his magic hammer Mjollnir.

Odin may have been the king of the gods, but his son Thor was just as highly honored. Thor had piercing eyes, a bristling red beard, and a lightning-quick temper. He was the strongest of all the gods, and the only god who never rode on horseback. Instead, Thor drove a chariot pulled by two huge goats. When he rode, lightning flashed from the goats' hooves, and the wheels of the chariot sounded like thunder.

Thor's greatest pleasure in life was battling giants. A number of myths recount his exploits in Jotunheim, the land of the giants, where he overcame great obstacles to defeat his foes. His favorite weapon was a magic hammer called **Mjollnir** ("Crusher"). When Thor hurled his red-hot hammer, it became a thunderbolt. Mjollnir never missed its mark, and it always returned to its owner.

The myth "Thor Loses His Hammer" is found in *Thrymskvida*, which translates to "The Poem of Thrym," composed in Iceland sometime between the tenth and early thirteenth centuries and preserved in the *Poetic Edda*. In *Thrymskvida*, the thunder god discovers that Thrym, king of the frost giants, has stolen Mjollnir. With Loki as his companion, Thor sets out for Jotunheim to recover his prized hammer. In order for his quest to succeed, the big, bearded, muscular god must disguise himself as a beautiful goddess. There are no special hidden meanings in this comical tale. The Norsemen told it just for fun.

Dramatis Personae

Thor God of thunder and lightning

Loki (LOW-kee) Trickster who lives in Asgard

Freyja (FRAY-yuh) Goddess of love and fertility

Thrym (THRIM) King of the frost giants

Thor And His Lost Hammer

One morning Thor awoke and rubbed the sleep from his eyes. He reached for his magic hammer. Mjollnir was gone!

With a roar that shook the nine worlds, Thor called for Loki. For once, though, the mischief-maker was innocent. Even Loki would not dare steal the mighty hammer that alone kept the terrible frost giants from storming Asgard.

Thor paced up and down, yanking his fiery red beard. Loki sat and pondered. At last, the clever trickster had an idea. "Only the giants could commit such a dastardly crime," he said. "I will ask Freyja for her magic falcon cloak, so that I may fly to Jotunheim and find the thief."

Thor and Loki hurried to Freyja's chambers. When the lovely goddess heard that Thor's hammer was missing, she turned pale with worry. Without hesitation, she wrapped her feathered cloak around Loki, transforming him into a falcon.

Swiftly the little bird winged its way to chilly Jotunheim. There Loki saw Thrym, king of the frost giants, sitting alone on a mountaintop.

"How are things in the land of gods?" asked the giant politely.

"Very bad," replied Loki. "Someone has stolen Thor's hammer."

"I stole the hammer," answered Thrym with an evil laugh that froze Loki to the marrow. "What's more, I have hidden it eight miles down in the earth, where no man or god shall ever find it. If Thor wants to see his precious Mjollnir again, he must send me fair Freyja as my wife."

In a whirl of feathers, Loki raced back to Asgard with the news. Again, he and Thor hurried to Freyja's chambers. This time, the goddess was not so cooperative. In fact, when she heard Thrym's proposal, she flew into a rage. Never never NEVER would Freyja marry that big, ugly giant!

Now all the Aesir gathered together to discuss the perilous situation. They turned over one plan after another. Finally, they came up with a solution. They would dress Thor as a bride and send him in place of Freyja.

"I won't do it!" Thor howled. "I will look like a sissy!" But the gods and goddesses ignored his protests. Struggling to hide their smiles, they bundled the burly thunder god into a wedding dress. They slipped gold bands on his hairy arms and clasped Freyja's jeweled necklace around his thick neck. A long white bridal veil covered his beard. A pretty cap topped his shaggy head. Loki gleefully dressed up as the maid to the blushing bride. Then off the pair went in Thor's goat-drawn chariot.

Thunder shook the mountains and fire split the clouds as Thor's chariot drew near Jotunheim. When

Freyja, the goddess of love and fertility, rides her cat-pulled wagon.

Thrym heard the racket, he shouted for his servants. "Make haste and prepare a great feast," the giant ordered joyfully. "The gods have sent the greatest of all treasures, fair Freyja, to be my wife!"

Soon, the happy groom escorted his bride to the banquet hall. He watched in pride as the veiled maiden took her seat among the giant guests at the table. Then his jaw dropped. His future wife had grabbed an entire ox! After gobbling that down, she ate eight whole salmon and all the other dainties prepared for the ladies, washing down the feast with three vats of **mead**.

> They bundled Thor in bridal linen … and wrapped his knees in skirts.
>
> ~ Thrymskvida, The *Poetic Edda*

Thor's Blessings

Thor was the most popular of all the Norse gods. The early Scandinavians prayed and made sacrifices to ensure his blessings on their homes, crops, and families. Many men and women showed their devotion to the hammer-wielding god by wearing miniature metal hammers on chains around their necks. A sacred hammer or the sign of the hammer was also used to bless brides, newborn children, and the dead. In addition, Thor was honored with statues in many temples built during Viking times. *Flateyjarbók* ("Flat Island Book"), a collection of dramatic tales written in Iceland in the late 1300s, describes a statue of the beloved god found at a temple in Norway.

> Thor sat in the middle. He was the most highly honored. He was huge and all adorned with gold and silver. Thor was arranged to sit in a chariot; he was very splendid. There were goats, two of them, harnessed in front of him, very well wrought. Both car and goats ran on wheels. The rope round the horns of the goats was of twisted silver, and the whole was worked with extremely fine craftsmanship.

"Who has ever seen a maiden with such hunger and thirst?" the giant asked in amazement.

"It is a sign of her passion," said Loki the bridesmaid in a high, squeaky voice. "My mistress was so eager for the wedding that she has not eaten a morsel in eight days."

Hearing that, the giant grew more excited than ever. He bent toward his bride and lifted a corner of her veil for a kiss. With a gasp, Thrym jumped back as if struck by a thunderbolt. "Freyja's eyes are so bright and fierce," he cried. "They seem to burn like fire!"

"It is a sign of her desire," said the clever bridesmaid. "My mistress was so eager for the wedding that she has not slept in eight nights."

Now Thrym practically swooned with love for his remarkable bride. He called for his servants to bring forth Mjollnir, for all proper weddings must be blessed with Thor's hammer. "Lay the hammer in the maiden's lap," cried the king of the giants, "to seal our marriage oaths and ensure blessings on our union."

Mjollnir was brought from its hiding place. When Thor felt his trusty hammer in his lap, his heart leaped within him. Thrym reached for his bride's hand. He got the surprise of his life when a big hairy arm loomed up over his head, swinging the weapon. Thor tore off his veil and cracked the giant's skull with the hammer. He sang as he clobbered all the other guests at the bridal banquet. Then Thor and Loki strode to the chariot and drove back to Asgard, where all the gods and goddesses sighed in relief at the sight of the precious hammer.

Monstrous Offspring

Thor battles the Midgard Serpent.

In many other myths of the Norsemen, gods used their strength and wits to triumph over the frost giants. However, the gods did not always win their battles. The Norsemen also told a number of tragic tales in which the gods suffered losses. One of the best known of these darker myths was the story of Fenrir the wolf. Snorri Sturluson's *Prose Edda* is the only complete account of this sad tale.

According to Snorri, a lady giant once caught the eye of Loki the trickster. From Loki's union with the giantess came three monstrous children: an immense snake called the Midgard Serpent, a hideous woman called Hel, and the fierce wolf Fenrir. In time Fenrir grew so huge and powerful that no ordinary chain could bind him. The gods obtained a magic bond to control the menacing beast. They managed to place the chain on Fenrir, but Tyr, god of war, lost his hand in the process.

Wolves were an ever-present danger in the lives of the early Scandinavians, so it is not surprising that they play a role in the Norse myths. As the most terrible of all the mythological wolves, Fenrir represents the destructive forces of nature. Raised among the gods in Asgard, he is also a symbol of the hatred, greed, and violence that can reside within the self. By enabling his fellow gods to restrain Fenrir, Tyr saves the world from destruction. He also saves the gods from the dark forces that can corrupt from within, overpowering reason and destroying the spirit. Tyr's actions reflect the highest ideals of the Norse warrior. He faces his enemy with courage and endures the loss of his hand without complaint. But the gods' victory is just one battle in a long war. According to prophecies, Fenrir will break his bonds and fight on the side of the giants in the final battle of Ragnarok.

Dramatis Personae

Loki (LOW-kee) Trickster who lives in Asgard

Odin (OH-din) King of the gods

Midgard Serpent Giant serpent who encircles the Earth

Hel Goddess of death and the underworld

Fenrir (FEN-rir) Giant wolf fathered by Loki

Tyr (TEER) God of war and justice

Frey (FRAY) God of sunshine, rain, peace, prosperity, and the harvest

Skirnir (SKEER-nir) Frey's servant

How Fenrir the Wolf Was Bound

One day disturbing news reached Asgard. Loki the trickster had fathered three children in the land of the frost giants. The first was a snapping wolf cub. The second was a spitting serpent. The third was a grim-looking hag whose body was half pink and wholesome, half black and decayed.

Now, Loki was trouble enough by himself. What evil might arise from his monstrous children? In search of an answer, the gods traveled to the home of the Norns, beside the Spring of Destiny, in the shadow of the World Tree. What the three maidens told them was anything but reassuring. For it was destined that Loki's children would bring the gods terrible harm and sorrow.

As soon as they heard the Norns' prophecy, the gods captured the three young monsters. Odin flung the serpent into the sea that surrounded Midgard, where it grew so large that it encircled the entire world of humans. Next, the king of gods cast the hag down into the dark underworld. There she became known as Hel, queen of the dead. From then on, the souls of all who died of sickness, accident, or old age instead of glorious battle went to Hel's dreary domain. There, they dined in her hall Damp-with-Sleet, at a table called Hunger, surrounded by tapestries called Glimmering Misfortune.

Finally, Odin turned to the wolf cub Fenrir. The Norns had said that this beast was the most dangerous of Loki's children. Therefore, Odin decided that the wolf should be raised in Asgard, where the gods could keep an eye on him.

It was not long before Odin began to regret his decision. Within a day, the cub was the size of a full-grown wolf. Within a week, his huge head towered over the golden rooftops of Asgard. The beast snarled and flashed his massive fangs whenever anyone approached him. Soon, none of the gods dared to feed him, except Odin's brave son Tyr. Each day, Tyr gave Fenrir huge joints of meat, which the greedy wolf devoured, bones and all. And each day, Fenrir grew larger and stronger and more ferocious.

The gods had to find a way to restrain Fenrir before it was too late. So they made a heavy brass chain and asked the wolf to try it on as a test of his strength. With a sneer, the monster agreed. The moment the gods bound him, he stretched and easily broke

> They made a very strong fetter … and brought it before the Wolf, bidding him try his strength.
>
> ~ Snorri Sturluson, The *Poetic Edda*

The Aesir throw a chain around the neck of Fenrir.

the chain. Next, the gods forged a massive iron chain, with links twice as strong as the first. Again they challenged Fenrir, declaring that anyone strong enough to break such a chain would gain fame throughout the nine worlds. Fenrir allowed the gods to bind him. This time he had to strain and struggle, but again he shattered the chain.

At last, the gods realized that no ordinary chain could bind Fenrir. So Odin sent Frey's servant Skirnir down to the world of the dwarfs. Those cunning craftsmen fashioned a chain from six things: the sound of a cat's footsteps, the beard of a maiden, the roots of a mountain, the timidity of a bear, the voice of a fish, and the spit of a bird. The magic chain was as smooth and soft as a silk ribbon. But because it was made from ingredients that were not of this world, no power in the world could break it.

As soon as Skirnir returned with the magic cord, the gods took it to Fenrir. They challenged the wolf to once again prove his might. But this time Fenrir refused to

Dwarf Magic

In Norse mythology, a race of dwarfs lived underground in a land called Nidavellir, or "Dark Fields." Famed far and wide for their craftsmanship, the dwarfs made many fabulous treasures for the gods. In this passage from the *Prose Edda*, a dwarf named Eitri is hard at work forging Thor's famous hammer. His brother Brokk, who is working the bellows that fan the furnace fire, is tormented by a fly. The pest is none other than Loki, who has bet his head that Eitri will not complete his task. Although Loki loses the bet, he manages to save his head. In the end, though, the dwarf has the last laugh.

> Then [Eitri] put iron in the furnace and told [Brokk] to blow, and said that everything would be spoiled if the bellows stopped working. ... The fly settled between [Brokk's] eyes and stung him on the eyelids so that the blood ran into his eyes and he could not see at all. He stopped the bellows and as quickly as possible brushed the fly away with one hand. At that moment the smith came in and said that everything in the furnace had been within an ace of being spoiled. Then he took from the forge a hammer. ...
>
> [The gods] decided that [Eitri] had won the wager. Then Loki offered to redeem [buy back] his head but the dwarf said that he could not expect to do that. "Catch me, then!" said Loki, and when the dwarf tried to seize him he was already a long way off... Then the dwarf asked Thor to catch him and he did so. The dwarf wanted to cut off his head, but Loki said he had a claim on his head but not his neck. The dwarf took a thong [leather cord] and a knife and ... sewed up [Loki's] mouth.

be bound. The silken ribbon looked so slender and weak that no fame would come from breaking it. In fact, it looked so flimsy that Fenrir suspected a trick.

"If that cord has been made by magic," said the wolf, "it will never come off, slender though it may look."

"Very well, don't try it," said Odin with a scornful smile. "There is no shame in being afraid of the gods."

The wolf laid back his ears and growled. "I am no coward," he snarled. "I will let you bind me with that cord, but only if one of you puts his hand between my jaws as a sign of your good faith."

> [Tyr] is most daring, and best in stoutness of heart.
>
> ~ Snorri Sturluson, The *Poetic Edda*

The gods looked at the wolf's long, sharp fangs. They looked at each other and shook their heads. Then, without a word, Tyr stepped forward, put out his right hand, and placed it in the wolf's mouth.

At once the gods wrapped the silken cord around Fenrir's neck and legs. The wolf began to struggle. The more he stretched and strained, the tighter the magic band became. Fenrir knew he was trapped. His eyes flashed with fury. All the gods laughed with relief—all except Tyr. He lost his hand.

When Fenrir opened his bloodstained jaws for another bite, one of the gods stuck in a sword. The hilt rested in the wolf's lower jaw, and the point in the roof of his mouth.

Once they were sure that Fenrir could not break away, the gods tied one end of the magic chain to a giant boulder and shoved the rock deep down into the earth. There the wolf was trapped. He would lie, howling through his gag, until Ragnarok, the end of the world.

PART 2: Stories and Myths

The Thaw of Spring

Frey, one of the fertility gods, sits on Odin's throne.

While the most well-known stories involve the gods at odds with the frost giants, in truth the relationship between the gods and giants was not always hostile. Several Norse myths speak of gods and giants in terms of friendship, attraction, and even love. The best stories, however, had both. Both conflict and love play a part in the story of Frey and Gerd.

Frey was one of the Vanir, or fertility gods, who came to live with the Aesir after the great war of the gods. According to mythology, he had a wonderful horse that could leap through fire unharmed, and a magic, shining sword that fought giants by itself. But he gave up both of these treasures for the love of the giant maiden Gerd.

Frey had seen the beautiful but coldhearted Gerd from afar and fallen in love with her. He sent his faithful servant Skirnir to the world of the giants to win the maiden's heart. Skirnir tried to bribe Gerd with wonderful gifts. When that failed, he resorted to increasingly nasty threats. At last, the giantess agreed to meet Frey in a sacred grove in nine nights' time and become his bride.

To the Norsemen, the myth of Frey and Gerd affirmed the natural order of the world. At the story's end, the beautiful giantess moves from the evil and chaotic world of the giants to the orderly world of the gods. According to some interpretations, the myth also may have explained the warming of the earth by the sun in springtime. Gerd, whose name means "Fenced-In," represents a wintry field. Through his messenger Skirnir, or "Shining," Frey sends the spring sun. Frey's love eventually melts the maiden's heart, just as the sun's rays thaw the frozen earth.

Our retelling of the story of Frey and Gerd is based on two sources: the tenth-century poem *För Skírnis* (translated to "Skirnir's Journey") from the *Poetic Edda* and Snorri Sturluson's *Prose Edda*.

Dramatis Personae

Frey (FRAY) God of sunshine, rain, peace, prosperity, and the harvest

Njord (NYURD) God of the sea

Gymir (GIH-mir) Giant father of Gerd

Skirnir (SKEER-nir) Frey's servant

Gerd Giantess who marries Frey

The Love of Frey and Gurd

Frey, son of Njord, knew that no one was allowed on Odin's high seat except the king of gods and his queen. Still, the young god could not help wondering what it would be like to sit on that exalted seat and look out over all the nine worlds. One day, Frey's curiosity got the better of him. He sneaked into the great god's hall and sat himself down on the throne.

How wonderful to see so clearly and so far! Frey turned his eyes to the frozen north and gasped as the land of the giants came into view. There on a mountaintop was the dwelling of the terrible giant Gymir. A beautiful young giantess was walking up a path to the hall. When the maiden raised her snow-white arms to open the door, her dazzling beauty lighted up the sky. Frey's heart swelled with longing. He rose and wandered home in a

Frey's servant Skirnir brings a message to win Gerd's love.

daze, so sick with love that he knew he had been well punished for sitting on Odin's throne.

For many long days, Frey moped in his hall. Sunlight faded from the earth, and crops thirsted for rain. The gods grew more and more worried. Finally, Njord summoned his son's trusted servant Skirnir and asked him to seek out the cause of Frey's unhappiness.

> Apples all-golden I have here eleven: these I will give thee, Gerd, thy love to gain.
>
> ~ *För Skírnis*, The *Poetic Edda*

Skirnir hastened to Frey's chambers. "Why do you sit here, alone and downcast?" he asked his master.

"I have seen a maiden dear to me, and I cannot live without her," the god groaned. "But I know my love is hopeless, for she is Gerd, Gymir's daughter, and her heart is surely as cold as winter."

"Do not despair," said Skirnir. "Though the journey to Jotunheim is long and dangerous, I will go there and woo the maiden for you. Only give me your horse that rides through fire and your gleaming sword that fights by itself."

Frey gladly granted Skirnir's wishes. Riding the wonderful horse and armed with the magic sword, the messenger fought his way through dark valleys and flickering flames to Jotunheim. At last he saw the hall of Gerd, Gymir's daughter. Huge hounds guarded the gates, snapping and howling like the chill winds of winter.

From inside her chambers, Gerd heard the racket. "What noise is that?" she asked her maidservant. "The ground shakes, and the house around me trembles."

"A man is riding up to the gates," said the servant. "He leaps from his horse. He draws near your father's fierce hounds."

"Bid the brave stranger enter, and offer him mead," ordered the fair giant maiden.

So Skirnir passed by the terrible hounds and entered Gerd's ice-cold chambers. He wasted no time getting to his errand. "I serve Frey, lord of sunshine and life-giving rain," he told Gymir's daughter. "I will give you eleven golden apples if you will marry my master."

"You cannot buy me with apples," said the maiden in a voice as cold as snow. "There are treasures enough in my father's house, and I do not love your master."

Skirnir offered Gerd a wonderful gold ring, which spun off eight more rings just like it every ninth night.

"You cannot buy me with rings," said the maiden in a voice as hard as ice. "I have all the gold I need in my father's house, and I do not love your master."

Then Skirnir grew angry. He flourished Frey's shining sword. "Do you see what I hold in my hand?" he shouted. "I will cut off your head if you do not obey my master's summons."

"You cannot sway me with force," said the proud giant maiden. "You had best leave, before my father finds you here and slays you."

Now Skirnir used his last and most terrible weapon. Carving three magic runes on his staff, he pronounced the curse that would fall on Gerd if she persisted in her defiance. "The wrath of the gods be upon you," cried the shining messenger. "You shall dwell alone at the edge of heaven and gaze on Hel's gates forever. Your meat will taste vile. Filth will be your only drink. Your skin will rot away, and men will view you with loathing. Never shall you know a husband, though you go mad with loneliness and longing."

Shaken by the dreadful curse, Gerd filled a frosty cup with mead. Shedding icy tears, she offered it to Skirnir. "Find welcome here instead," said the giant maiden, "and a heart willing for your master."

Then Skirnir lowered his staff and erased the curse. Gerd pledged to meet Frey after nine nights, in the sacred forest of Barri ("Barley"). Joyfully, the messenger rode home and found his anxious master waiting. He told Frey the glad tidings. But instead of rejoicing, the god moaned, "Nine nights! How shall I bear to wait when my heart is so filled with desire?"

On the ninth night, after being driven mad with waiting, Frey came to the forest of Barri. The frost maiden kept her promise, but feared meeting a man she did not love. When Gerd entered the sacred grove and saw her intended husband, the warmth of his love melted her cold heart. They married, and Gerd took her seat beside Frey in Asgard, where they dwelled together in happiness. As Gerd's heart had melted, so had the hard winds of winter, and on earth the winter thawed, and people enjoyed a season of fine weather, rich harvests, and peace.

PART 2: Stories and Myths

Balder's Death and the Doom of the Gods

This engraving depicts Balder, the god of light, innocence, joy, purity, and beauty.

Unlike in many religions, the Norse gods were not **immortal** and could die. In fact, it was their destiny. All of the episodes of Norse mythology lead up to Ragnarok, or "Doom of the Gods." The death of the gods will be brought about by the actions of Loki the trickster.

In the earlier myths, Loki gets the gods in and out of trouble with his mischievous pranks. At heart, though, Loki is evil. By allowing this evil to remain in their midst, the gods end up losing their greatest treasure and sealing their doom.

The great treasure of the gods is Balder, pure and radiant lord of light and innocence. Jealousy leads Loki to trick Balder's blind brother, Hod, into causing the beloved god's death. Balder's downfall is a sign of the coming of Ragnarok. During this final battle between good and evil, the gods die fighting their ancient foes, and the whole Earth is destroyed. But as foretold in prophecies, a new world cleansed of all evil is reborn from the destruction.

The myths of Balder's death and Ragnarok are told in a number of Norse poems and prose narratives. The early Scandinavians may have borrowed some elements of these tales from the peoples of other cultures, including the Persians of ancient Iran and the Celts of central and Western Europe. In addition, some scholars think that the Norse accounts of doomsday may have been influenced by the Christian vision of Judgment Day, as told in the book of Revelation. There are also distinctive features in the Norse myths that clearly reflect the land and character of early Scandinavia. Like the Norse creation story, Ragnarok takes place in a land of fire and flood. And like the ideal Scandinavian warrior, the gods face their enemies bravely, accepting their fate and laughing in the face of death.

Dramatis Personae

Balder (BAWL-der) God of light, innocence, joy, purity, and beauty

Odin (OH-din) King of the gods

Hel Goddess of death and the underworld

Hod (HAWD) Blind god of darkness

Frigg Wife of Odin; queen of the Aesir

Thor God of thunder and lightning

Loki (LOW-kee) Trickster who lives in Asgard

Fenrir (FEN-rir) Giant wolf fathered by Loki

Midgard Serpent Giant serpent who encircles the Earth

Surt Fire giant who rules Muspellheim, the land of fire

Heimdall (HAME-doll) Guardian of the bridge Bifrost

Tyr (TEER) God of war and justice

Frey (FRAY) God of sunshine, rain, peace, prosperity, and the harvest

Balder's Dreams

Balder, son of Odin, was the best of the gods. His beauty lit up the world, and his innocence and sweet disposition made all creation adore him. The gentle god lived in a fair hall called Broad-Gleaming, where no impure thoughts or visions ever crossed the threshold.

Then, one night, Balder began to have terrible dreams. Monsters chased him and threatened to cast him down into the darkness forever. When Balder told his father of his dreams, Odin was filled with foreboding. The king of gods saddled his wonderful eight-legged horse Sleipnir and rode down the long gloomy road to Hel's domain. Outside the gates, he disguised his features and used his powerful charms to call up the spirit of a long-dead wisewoman. Odin asked the prophetess why Hel's halls were hung with gold ornaments. "The hall is decked, the table set, the mead brewed to welcome Balder," said the dreadful spirit.

Odin's heart sank. "What demon shall steal the life from Odin's son?" he demanded.

"Balder's own brother, blind Hod, shall be his bane," she answered.

Then Odin roared with grief, and the spirit saw through his disguise. "Ride home, king of gods, and come here no more," she cried with cruel laughter. "For the hope of the Aesir is gone, and destruction comes to Asgard."

With that awful pronouncement, the spirit sank back into her grave. Odin returned to Asgard with a heavy heart. He knew that what was fated must come to pass, and nothing in heaven or Earth could stop it. But he could not bring himself to tell the gods and goddesses that they would lose their beloved Balder.

The Death of Balder

The Aesir were worried about Balder's nightmares. They feared that the dreams were an omen, a warning that the beloved god's life was in danger. While one god after another proposed plans to protect Balder, Odin sat silent. At last, Frigg declared that she knew a way to guard her son from peril.

Frigg traveled to every corner of the nine worlds, visiting anything that could bring danger. She spoke with fire, water, earth, stones, metals, trees, beasts, birds, snakes, poisons, and every kind of illness. Each of these agreed to swear an oath that it would never harm Balder.

After Frigg completed her task, the Aesir put it to the test. Balder stood in their midst, and someone tossed a pebble at him. The tiny missile stopped in midair and fell to the ground. Next, someone tossed a stick. It, too, fell harmlessly. Soon all the gods and goddesses were laughing merrily, enjoying their new game. One threw darts at the shining god. Another swung his sword. Thor even hurled his mighty hammer. No matter what they did, nothing could harm Balder.

But someone was not laughing. Loki the trickster sulked in a corner, jealousy gnawing at his black heart. The gods had been avoiding Loki, blaming him for all their troubles. Now they had the nerve to make a fuss over their golden-haired darling! Slipping away unnoticed, Loki transformed himself into a haggard old woman and hobbled over to Frigg's hall. "Do you hear that laughter?" he asked the goddess in a raspy old voice. "I wonder what the Aesir are up to."

"They are playing games with my son Balder," Frigg answered happily. "All the world loves him, and nothing can harm him."

"Nothing, good mother?" asked the old hag. "Has everything sworn an oath to spare him?"

Loki's Punishment

After Balder died, Hel declared that she would release the god from her grim domain if all creation wept for him. The Aesir sent messengers throughout the nine worlds. Men and beasts, fire and water, stones and metals all began weeping. Everything wept except one hard-hearted giantess, who turned out to be Loki in disguise. For this last act of treachery, the gods seized the trickster and bound him in a cave deep beneath the Earth.

This account of Loki's punishment comes from a prose note at the end of the tenth-century poem *Lokasenna*, or "Loki's Wrangling." The brief narrative mentions four little-known characters from Norse mythology: Loki's faithful wife, Sigyn; their two sons, Vali and Narfi; and Skadi, wife of the sea god Njord.

> Loki hid himself in [a] waterfall in the guise of a salmon, and there the gods took him. He was bound with the bowels of his son Vali, but his son Narfi was changed to a wolf. Skadi took a poison-snake and fastened it up over Loki's face, and the poison dropped thereon. Sigyn, Loki's wife, sat there and held a shell under the poison, but when the shell was full she bore away the poison, and meanwhile the poison dropped on Loki. Then he struggled so hard that the whole earth shook therewith.

"Everything but a little plant called mistletoe," said Frigg. "I found it growing on the trunk of an oak tree outside Odin's golden hall of Valhalla, but I thought it too young for oath taking."

Smiling slyly to himself, Loki bid the goddess good day. As he left her hall, he resumed his old form and hurried to Valhalla. There he found the mistletoe, just as Frigg had described it. He plucked a small sprig and sharpened it into a dart. Then he hurried back to the merry circle in Asgard. He sidled up to the blind god Hod, who stood apart from the others. "Why aren't you throwing things at your brother like everyone else?" asked Loki.

"Because I can't see him," Hod explained patiently. "Besides, I have no weapon."

"Here, take this little twig," said Loki. "I will show you where Balder is standing."

So Hod took his place among the gods and aimed where Loki directed. The sharp dart flew through the air. It pierced Balder through the heart. The golden god fell dead to the ground.

There was a moment of shocked silence. Then all the gods and goddesses began weeping. None was more overcome with grief than Odin. He alone knew what the loss of his dearest son meant for the Aesir. For Odin had looked into the future, and he knew that Balder's death was the first sign of Ragnarok.

Balder was killed by a sharpened twig of mistletoe.

Endings and Beginnings

After the death of Balder, light and innocence left the earth. Brother killed brother, father slew son, and sons rose up against their fathers. Everywhere was sin and misery, until Midgard ran red with blood. Then the gods knew that the prophecies of old were about to be fulfilled. Ragnarok was at hand.

> Axe-time, sword-time,
> shields are sundered,
> Wind-time, wolf-time,
> ere the world falls.
>
> ~ *Voluspa*,
> The *Poetic Edda*

As had been foretold, the earth endured three years of winter without end. Snows fell, winds howled, and frost hardened the ground. Sun and Moon looked fearfully over their shoulders, and the wolves that had long pursued them caught and devoured them. The stars vanished from the darkened sky. The earth groaned and shuddered, until the trees were uprooted and great mountains tumbled down.

As the frozen earth cracked open, all bonds were broken. The wolf Fenrir escaped from his long imprisonment. His eyes blazed with fire, and his huge mouth gaped open, with the lower jaw scraping the ground and the upper jaw pressed against the sky. The Midgard Serpent rose from the sea and slithered onto land, spitting poison. The sky burst asunder and out rode the giants, led by Surt and his bright sword of fire. The gates of Hel opened and the dead rose in arms, with Loki as their leader.

From his post beside Bifrost, Heimdall saw the evil hosts advance on Asgard. He blew his great horn, calling the Aesir to the final battle. At that stirring sound, the gods sprang from their golden halls, strapped on their armor, and mounted their warhorses. Swiftly they galloped over the rainbow bridge, shouting their brave battle cries.

> In wondrous beauty once again shall the golden tables stand mid the grass
>
> ~ *Voluspa*, The *Poetic Edda*

The two armies met on the vast plain called Vigrid, or "Battle Surge." There, mighty Odin fought Fenrir but was swallowed up by the monster-wolf's jaws. Thor slew the Midgard Serpent, then staggered and fell, killed by the serpent's poisonous breath. Tyr died battling the hounds of Hel. Heimdall battled with Loki, and each killed the other. Frey struggled with Surt and died. Then Surt flung his fiery sword. The whole world was engulfed in flames, and the Earth sank into the boiling sea.

For long ages, all was dark and silent. Then one day, a new Earth rose from the sea. It was green and fair, bursting with fruit and grain and flowers. A man and a woman emerged from beneath the roots of the sacred tree Yggdrasil, where they had sheltered while the earth burned. Nourished on the morning dews, they would people the world, and all would live together in perfect peace and happiness.

At last Balder rose from the dark underworld. The land he knew had been destroyed. He journeyed to the ruins of Asgard, where he met his brother Hod and four youths who had escaped the devastation. The small group of gods walked the green new grass of heaven, remembering days long past. They thought of Loki and his terrible offspring Fenrir and the Midgard Serpent. They spoke of frost giants, good and evil. But the young gods were not ones to wallow in the past. Instead, they focused on wonderful tales of the old gods and goddesses: of Tyr the brave and Frey the good, of Idun's golden apples and Thor's powerful hammer, and of Odin, the all-father, wisest of all.

GLOSSARY

Aesir (AY-zir) The main group of Norse gods, which included Odin and Thor. The Aesir were gods of war and destiny.

archaeologists Scientists who study the physical remains of past cultures to learn about human life and activity.

Asgard The world of the gods, which floated on a plain far above the world of humans.

Bifrost The rainbow bridge connecting Asgard and Midgard.

deity A god, goddess, or other divine being.

Germanic peoples A major group of related tribes who lived in Scandinavia and Germany as early as 1000 BCE and spread across much of Europe. The Germanic peoples spoke variations on a language known as Germanic, which developed into English, German, Dutch, and several Scandinavian languages.

immortal Living forever.

Jotunheim The land of the giants.

mead A sweet alcoholic beverage made from honey, water, grain, and yeast.

Midgard The world of human beings.

Mjollnir The magic war hammer of Thor. Mjollnir means "Crusher."

Muspellheim The world of fire, ruled by the fire giant Surt.

mythology The whole body of myths belonging to a people.

myths Traditional stories about gods and other divine beings, which were developed by ancient cultures to explain the mysteries of the physical and spiritual worlds.

Niflheim The ancient world of the dead.

Norns Three goddesses who spun a thread of life for every living being, determining its destiny from birth to death.

prophecy A foretelling of something that will happen in the future.

Ragnarok The final battle between gods and giants that would bring about the destruction of the world. Ragnarok means "Doom of the Gods."

runes Letters of an ancient alphabet used by a number of Germanic peoples, including the Vikings.

skalds Scandinavian poets who often traveled from court to court, composing verses in honor of the kings and chieftains.

Valhalla The golden hall of the god Odin, where the souls of fallen heroes dwelled after death. Valhalla means "Hall of the Slain."

Valkyries Mythical warrior maidens who met the souls of brave warriors who died in battle and led them to Valhalla.

Vanir The second of the two main groups of Norse gods. The Vanir, who included Njord, Frey, and Freyja, were gods of fertility and prosperity.

Yggdrasil The huge ash tree that bound the nine mythological worlds together; also known as the World Tree.

BIOGRAPHICAL DICTIONARY OF NORSE WRITERS

Our list of Norse writers is very short because the names of most of the early Scandinavian poets and storytellers have been forgotten. For centuries, Norse poems and stories about the gods were memorized and passed down orally rather than recorded in books. Many tales were probably lost forever. The two best surviving sources of the Norse myths are Snorri Sturluson's *Prose Edda* and the *Poetic Edda*.

The *Poetic Edda*

The *Poetic Edda* is a collection of thirty-four poems that were composed at various times between the ninth century and the mid-thirteenth century. The poems were collected and written down in Iceland sometime around the end of the thirteenth century. Our book includes references to four poems from the *Poetic Edda*: *Voluspa*, or "The Wise-Woman's Prophecy;" *Hávamál*, or "The Speech of the High One;" *För Skírnis*, or "Skirnir's Journey;" and *Lokasenna*, or "Loki's Wrangling."

Snorri Sturluson

circa 1179–1241 CE

Snorri Sturluson was an Icelandic political leader, historian, and poet. His writings are one of our most important sources of information on Norse mythology. His best-known works include *Heimskringla*, a collection of sagas on the lives of Norway's kings, and the *Prose Edda*. The *Prose Edda* contains Snorri's retellings of mythological tales as well as excerpts from traditional Scandinavian poetry.

Thjódólf of Hvin

circa 860–935 CE

The Norwegian poet Thjódólf of Hvin served as one of the skalds, or court poets, of King Harald Fairhair of Norway. Only two of his poems have survived: *Haustlöng* ("Autumn-Long") is a "shield poem," written in praise of the mythological scenes depicted on a battle shield. *Ynglingatal* ("The Tally of the Ynglings") blends fact and legends to celebrate the lives of King Harald's ancestors.

THE LIVING MYTHS

The Viking Age ended a thousand years ago, but Norse mythology has lived on. The tales of the early Scandinavians have influenced the work of writers, filmmakers, artists, and other creative people all around the world. Here are just a few of the many areas in which the myths of the Norsemen have touched our modern world.

Language
English words derived from Norse mythology include several days of the week: Tuesday ("Tyr's Day"), Wednesday ("Woden's [Odin's] Day"), Thursday ("Thor's Day"), and Friday ("Frigg's Day").

Literature

The Chronicles of Narnia (C. S. Lewis)

Dragonlance Chronicles Trilogy (Margaret Weis and Tracy Hickman)

Forgotten Realms: Icewind Dale Trilogy (R. A. Salvatore)

The Hobbit and *The Lord of the Rings* (J. R. R. Tolkien)

Legends of Lone Wolf series (Joe Dever and John Grant)

The Weirdstone of Brisingamen (Alan Garner)

The Wheel of Time series (Robert Jordan)

Wodan's Children series (Diana Paxson)

Movies

The Mask (1994)

The Lord of the Rings: The Fellowship of the Ring (2001), *The Two Towers* (2002), and *The Return of the King* (2003)

Chronicles of Narnia: The Lion, the Witch, and the Wardrobe (2005)

Thor (2011)

The Avengers (2012)

Thor: The Dark World (2013)

Avengers: Age of Ultron (2015)

Music

The Ring of the Nibelung (opera cycle, Richard Wagner)

FURTHER INFORMATION

Books

Auerbach, Loren, and Jacqueline Simpson. S*agas of the Norsemen: Viking and German Myth*. London: Duncan Baird Publishers, 1997.

Daly, Kathleen N. *Norse Mythology A to Z: A Young Reader's Companion*. Revised by Marian Rengel. New York: Facts on File, 2003.

d'Aulaire, Ingri, and Edgar Parin d'Aulaire. *d'Aulaires' Book of Norse Myths*. New York: New York Review of Books, 2005.

Hamilton, Edith. *Mythology: Timeless Tales of Gods and Heroes*. New York: Warner Books, 1999.

Lindow, John. *Norse Mythology: A Guide to Gods, Heroes, Rituals, and Beliefs*. New York: Oxford University Press, 2002.

Philip, Neil. *Odin's Family: Myths of the Vikings*. New York: Orchard Books, 1996.

Richards, Julian D. *The Vikings: A Very Short Introduction*. New York: Oxford University Press, 2005.

Schomp, Virginia. *The Vikings*. New York: Scholastic, 2005.

Sturluson, Snorri and Jesse L. Byock. *The Prose Edda: Norse Mythology.* New York: Penguin Classics, 2006.

Thorsson, Örnólfur, ed. *The Sagas of the Icelanders*. New York: Penguin Books, 2001.

Websites

Encyclopedia Mythica

www.pantheon.org/areas/mythology/europe/norse

This online encyclopedia contains more than 7,000 entries on the myths, folktales, and legends of many different cultures. There are 150 articles on the gods, monsters, heroes, worlds, and sources of the ancient Scandinavian myths.

The Online Medieval & Classical Library: The Story of the Volsungs

omacl.org/Volsunga

The Story of the Volsungs is one of the most exciting Norse legendary tales, recounting the adventures of the mighty hero Sigurd and the Valkyrie Brynhild. This electronic edition is based on the translation by William Morris and Eirikr Magnusson. The site also includes excerpts from the *Poetic Edda*.

The *Prose Edda*

www.sacred-texts.com/neu/pre

Snorri Sturluson's *Prose Edda* is one of our most important sources of information on the Norse gods and their adventures. This electronic edition is based on the translation by Arthur Gilchrist Brodeur.

Windows to the Universe: Norse Myths

www.windows2universe.org/mythology/worldmap_new.html

Presented by the University of Michigan, this award-winning site helps students and teachers explore the connections between Earth and space sciences and the Norse myths. The text is offered on three reading levels, for elementary, middle school, and high school students.

SELECTED BIBLIOGRAPHY

Bellows, Henry Adams, trans. *The Poetic Edda*. New York: American-Scandinavian Foundation, 1968.

Bulfinch, Thomas. *The Golden Age of Myth and Legend*. Hertfordshire, England: Wordsworth Reference, 1993.

Cotterell, Arthur. *Norse Mythology*. New York: Smithmark Publishers, 1997.

Crossley-Holland, Kevin. *The Norse Myths*. New York: Pantheon, 1980.

Davidson, H. R. Ellis. *Gods and Myths of the Viking Age*. New York: Barnes and Noble Books, 1996.

Grant, John. *An Introduction to Viking Mythology*. Secaucus, NJ: Chartwell Books, 2002.

Guerber, H. A. *Myths of the Norsemen: From the Eddas and Sagas*. New York: Dover, 1992.

Haywood, John. *Encyclopaedia of the Viking Age*. New York: Thames & Hudson, 2000.

Lindow, John. *Norse Mythology: A Guide to the Gods, Heroes, Rituals, and Beliefs.* New York: Oxford University Press, 2001.

Murray, Alexander S. *Manual of Mythology*. Edited by William H. Klapp. New York: Tudor, 1935.

Orchard, Andy. *Cassell Dictionary of Norse Myth and Legend.* London: Cassell, 1997.

Page, R. I. *Norse Myths*. Austin: University of Texas Press, 1993.

Sturluson, Snorri. *Prose Edda*. Translated by Jean I. Young. Berkeley, CA: University of California Press, 1964.

QUOTATION CITATIONS

Quoted passages in sidebars come from the following sources:

"The Sibling Sun and Moon," page 35; "The Norse Trickster Loki," page 41; and "Dwarf Magic," page 64, from Snorri Sturluson, The *Prose Edda*, translated by Jean I. Young (Berkeley, CA: University of California Press, 1964).

"Odin's Wisdom," page 51, from the *Poetic Edda*, translated by Benjamin Thorpe, at www.northvegr.org/lore/poetic2/006_07.php

"Thor's Blessings," page 57, from H. R. Ellis Davidson, *Gods and Myths of the Viking Age* (New York: Barnes and Noble Books, 1996).

"Loki's Punishment," page 78, from The *Poetic Edda*, translated by Henry Adams Bellows (New York: American-Scandinavian Foundation, 1968).

INDEX

Page numbers in **boldface** are illustrations. Entries in **boldface** are glossary terms.